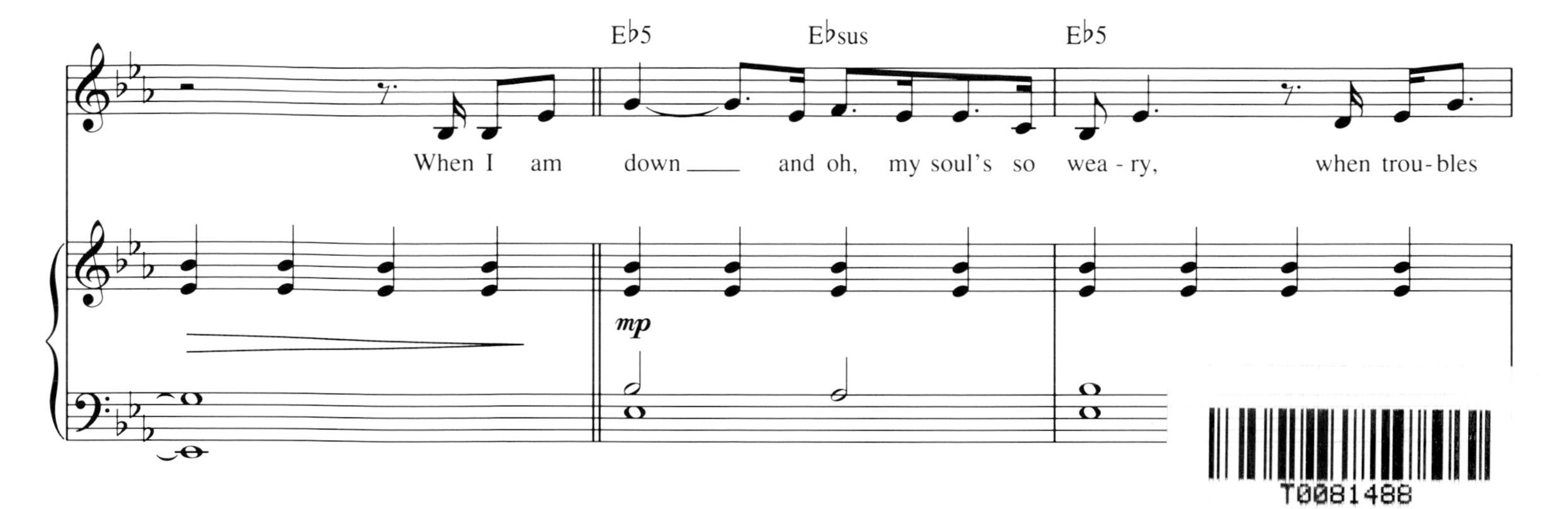
E♭5 E♭sus E♭5
When I am down and oh, my soul's so wea - ry, when trou - bles
mp
T0081488

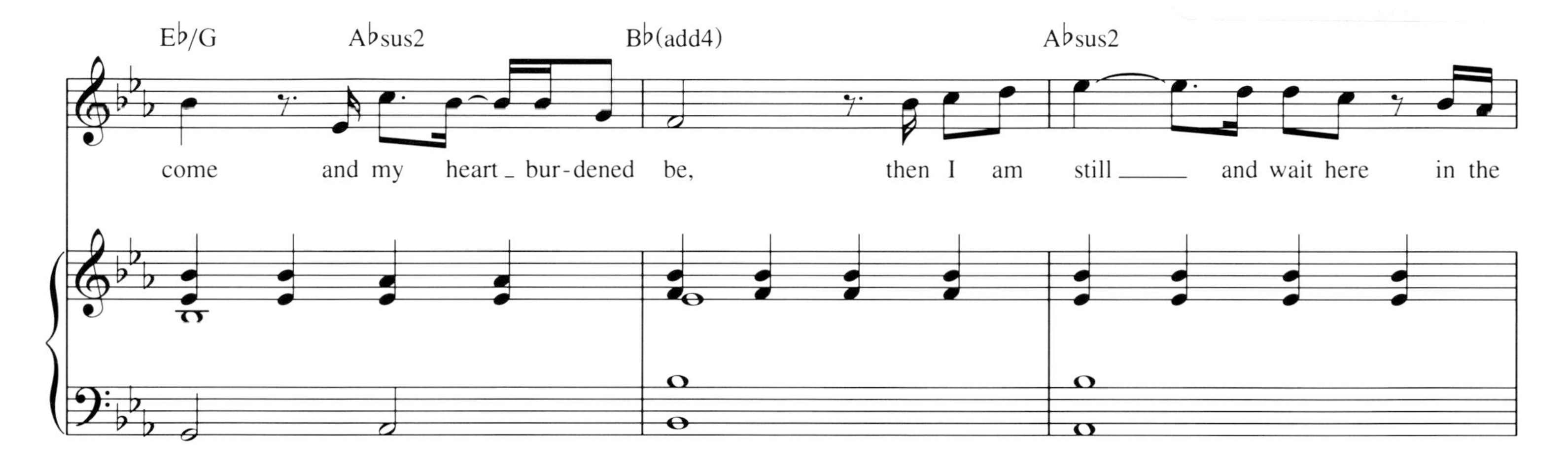
E♭/G A♭sus2 B♭(add4) A♭sus2
come and my heart _ bur - dened be, then I am still and wait here in the

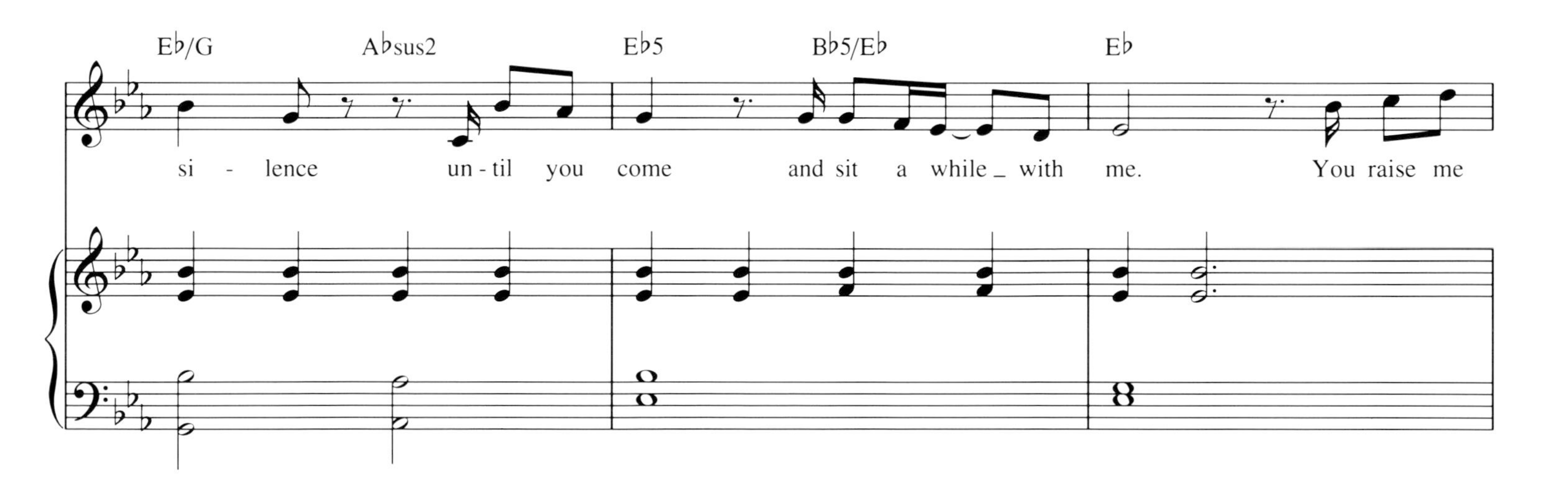
E♭/G A♭sus2 E♭5 B♭5/E♭ E♭
si - lence un - til you come and sit a while _ with me. You raise me

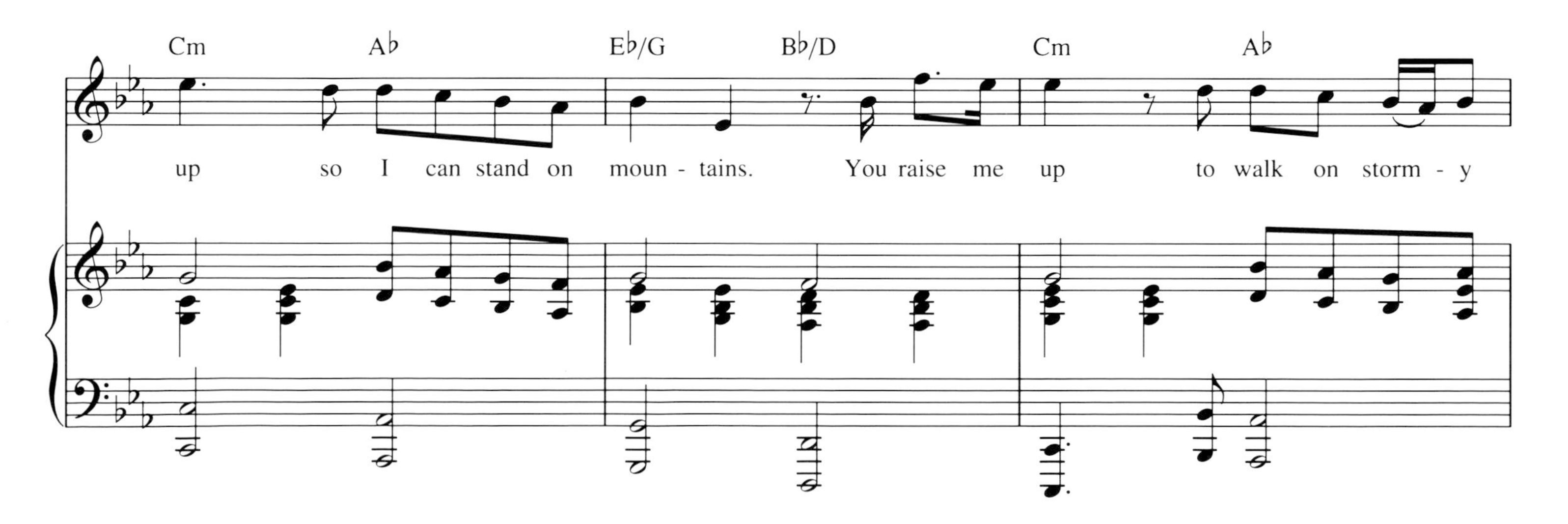
Cm A♭ E♭/G B♭/D Cm A♭
up so I can stand on moun - tains. You raise me up to walk on storm - y

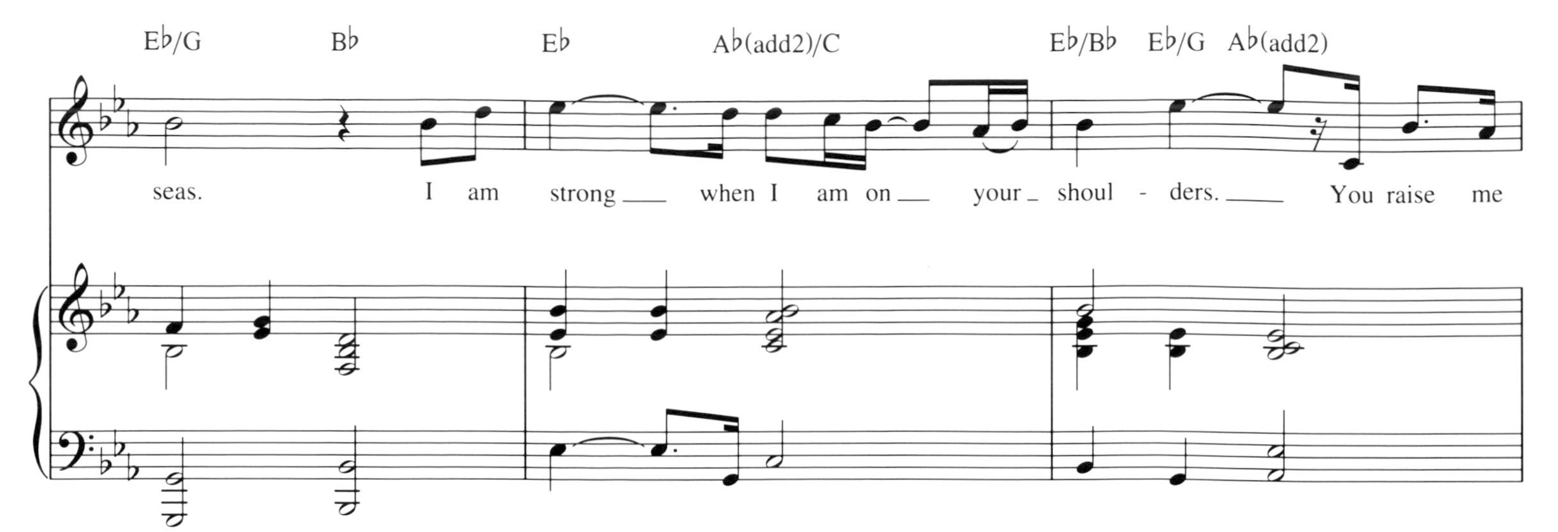
E♭/G
B♭
E♭
A♭(add2)/C
E♭/B♭
E♭/G
A♭(add2)
seas. I am strong when I am on your shoul - ders. You raise me

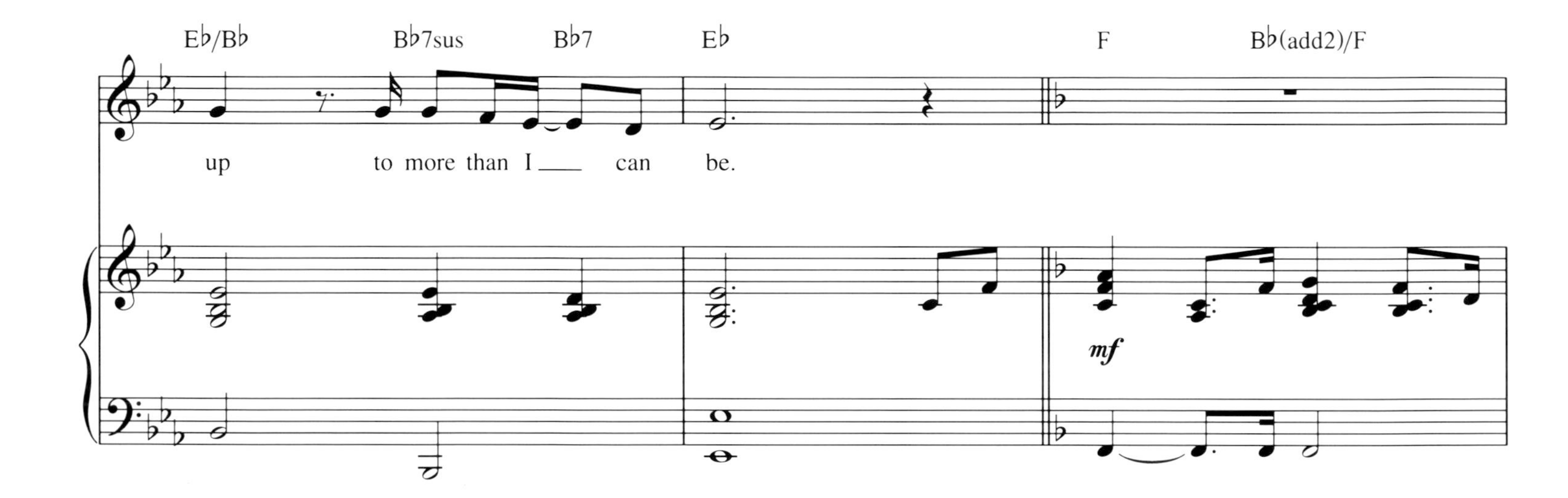
E♭/B♭
B♭7sus
B♭7
E♭
F
B♭(add2)/F
up to more than I can be.
mf

F
F(add2)/A
B♭
F/C
C
3

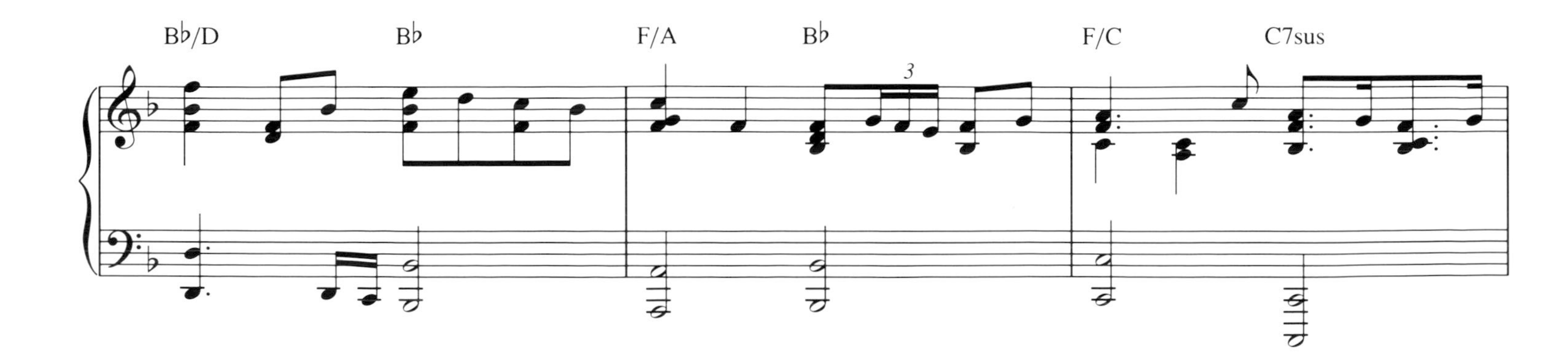
B♭/D
B♭
F/A
B♭
F/C
C7sus
3

YOU RAISE ME UP

Words and Music by BRENDAN GRAHAM
and ROLF LOVLAND

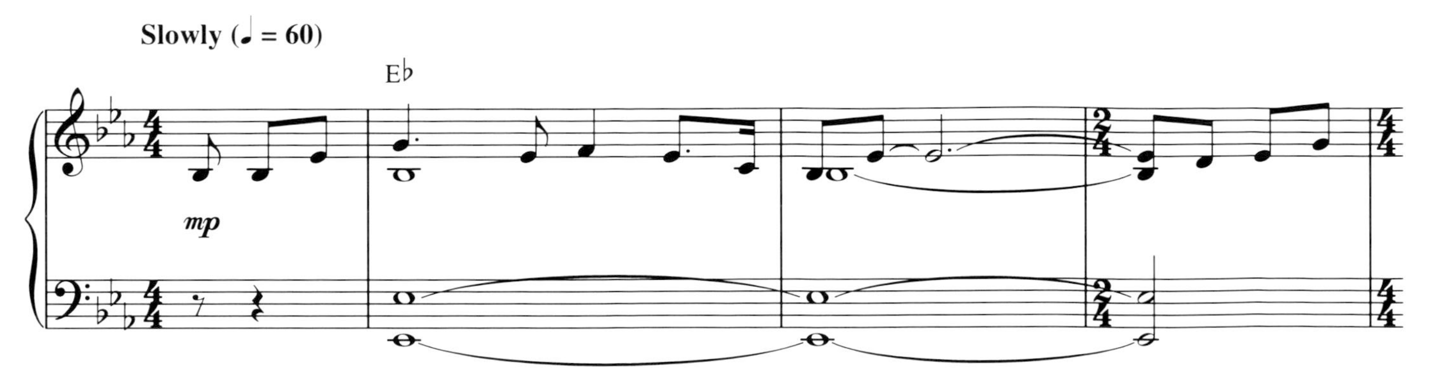

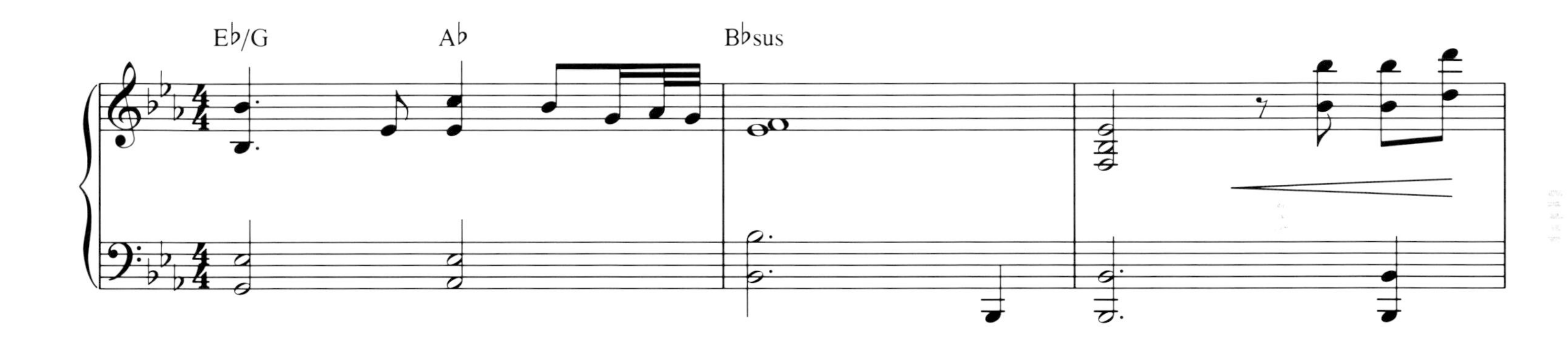

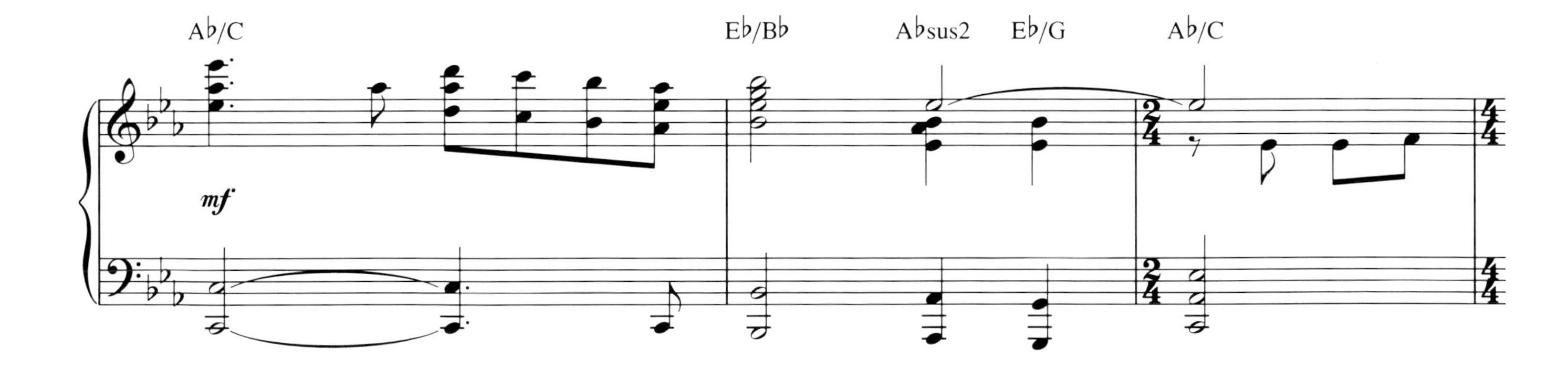

Vocal Solo with Piano Accompaniment & Orchestrated CD Accompaniment

You Raise Me Up

Words and Music by BRENDAN GRAHAM and ROLF LOVLAND

Recorded by
JOSH GROBAN
on REPRISE RECORDS

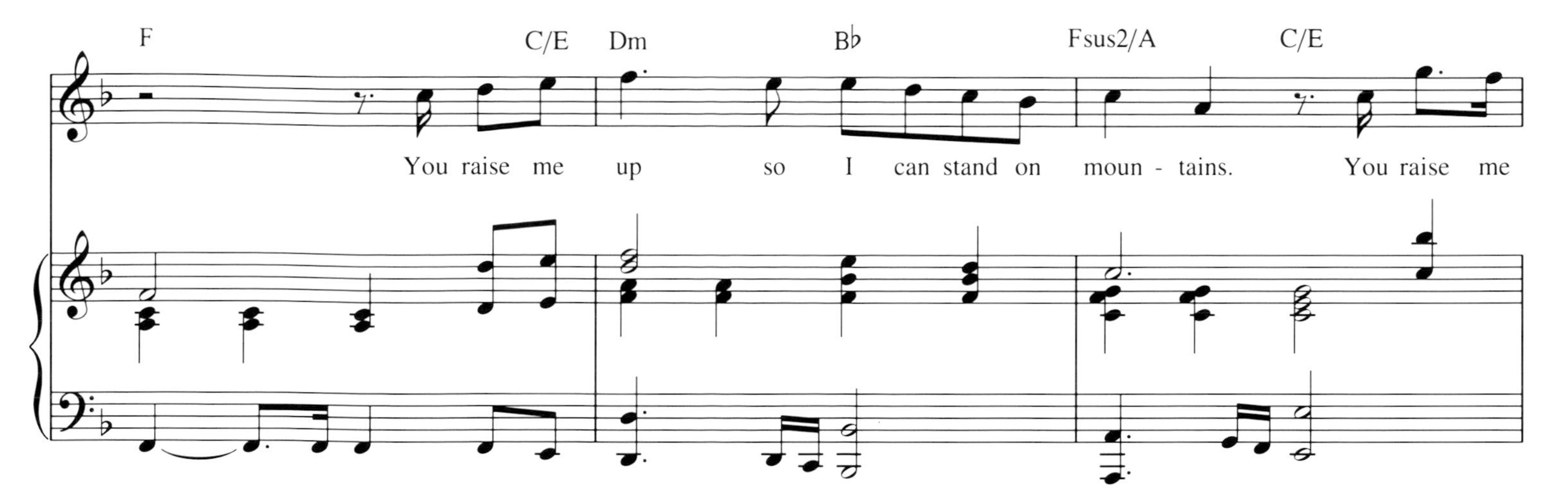
F C/E Dm B♭ Fsus2/A C/E
You raise me up so I can stand on moun - tains. You raise me

Dm B♭ F/C Csus C F5
up to walk on storm - y seas. I am strong when I am on your

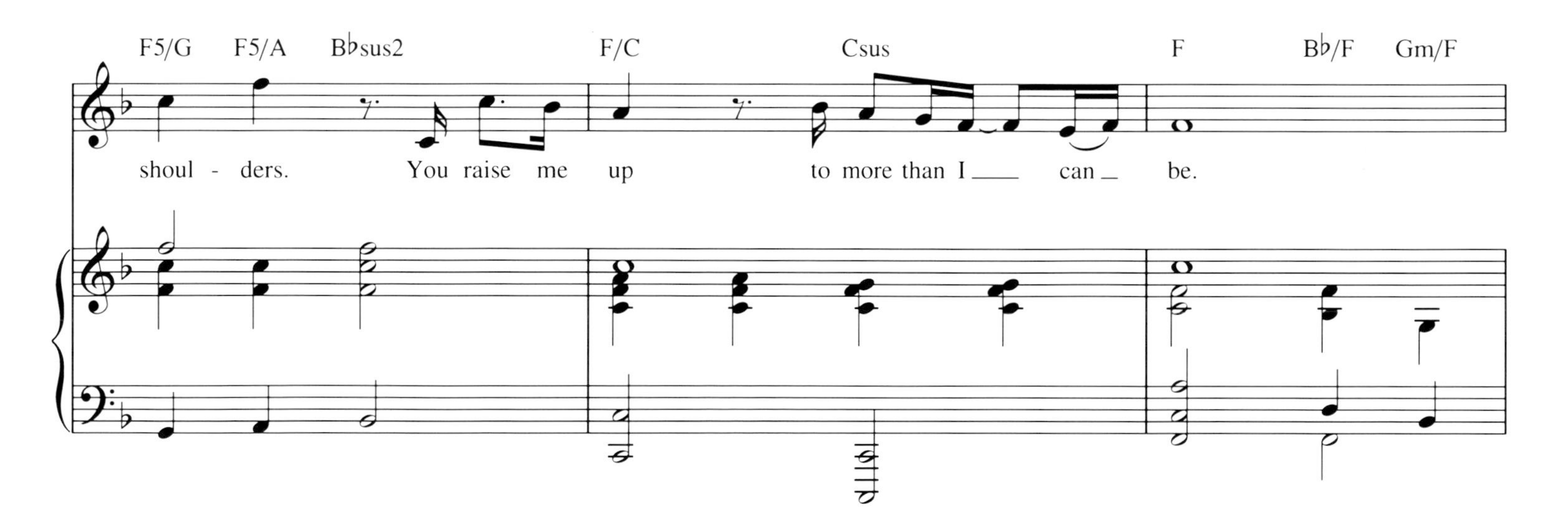
F5/G F5/A B♭sus2 F/C Csus F B♭/F Gm/F
shoul - ders. You raise me up to more than I can be.

F N.C. E♭m C♭
You raise me up so I can stand on
6
f

G♭/B♭
D♭/F
E♭m
C♭
moun - tains. You raise me up to walk on storm - y

G♭/D♭
D♭
G♭
C♭
seas. I am strong when I am on your

G♭
C♭sus2/E♭
G♭/D♭
D♭sus
shoul - ders. You raise me up to more than I can

G♭
B♭7/D
E♭m
C♭
be. You raise me up so I can stand on

G♭/B♭ D♭/F E♭m C♭ G♭/D♭ D♭
mountains. You raise me up to walk on storm - y seas. I am
dim.
8vb

G♭ E♭m7 G♭/D♭ D♭sus D♭
strong when I am on your shoul - ders. You raise me up to more than I can
mp

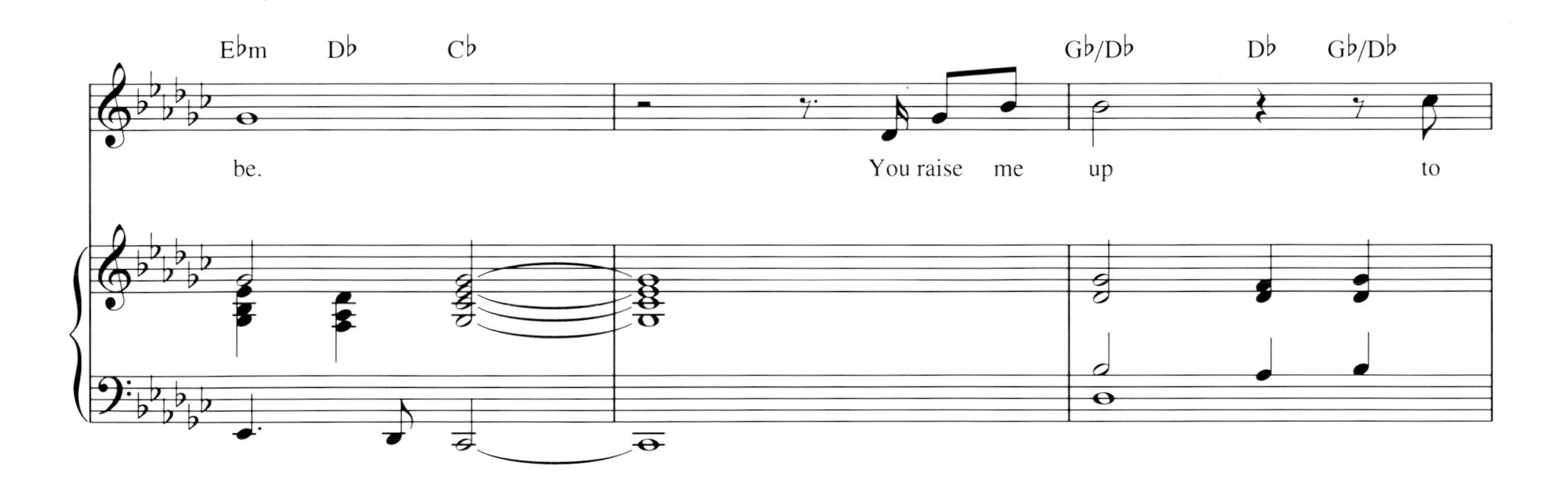
E♭m D♭ C♭ G♭/D♭ D♭ G♭/D♭
be. You raise me up to

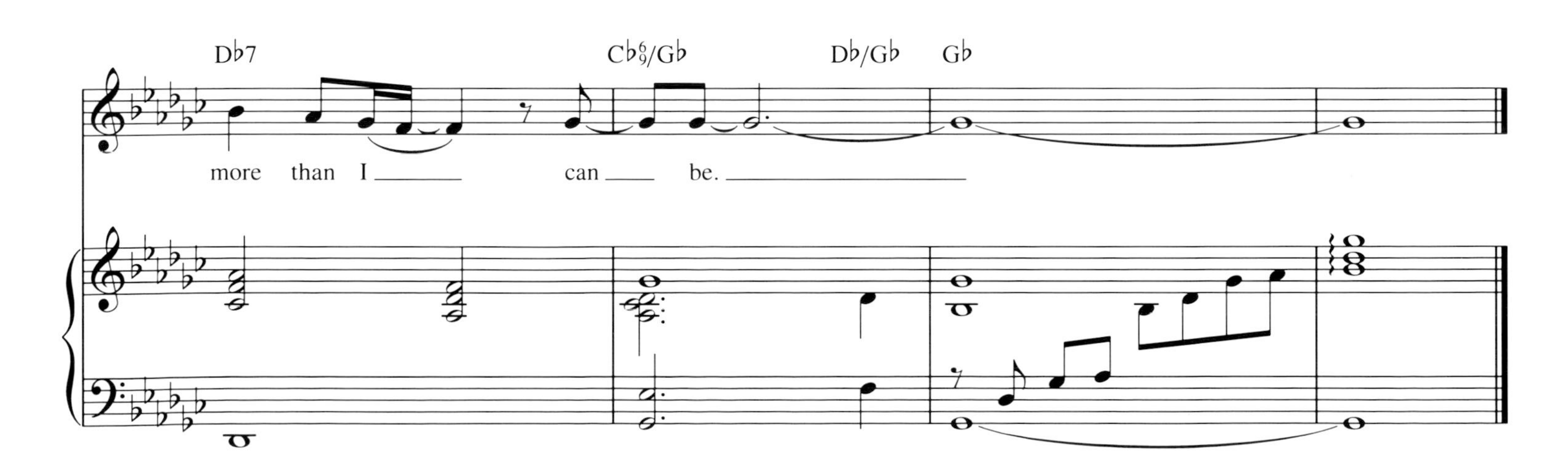
D♭7 D♭/G♭ G♭
more than I can be.